How to Be a
BETTY

How to Be a BETTY

The Ultimate Guide to Unleashing Your Inner

BOOP!

Sherrie Krantz

Ballantine Books ✦ New York

Author's Note: This book proposes a program of exercise recommendations for the reader to follow. However, you should consult a qualified medical professional (and, if you are pregnant, your ob/gyn) before starting this or any other fitness program. As with any diet or exercise program, if at any time you experience any discomfort, stop immediately and consult your physician.

For Amy . . .

xo

Contents

Introduction   1

Chapter One:
How to Glow Like Betty, and Then Some   5

Chapter Two:
How to Be a Betty at Work   31

Chapter Three:
How to Be a Betty in Love   47

Chapter Four:
How to Be a Betty with Friends   63

Chapter Five:
How to Be a Betty at Home and with Your Family   71

How to Be a
BETTY

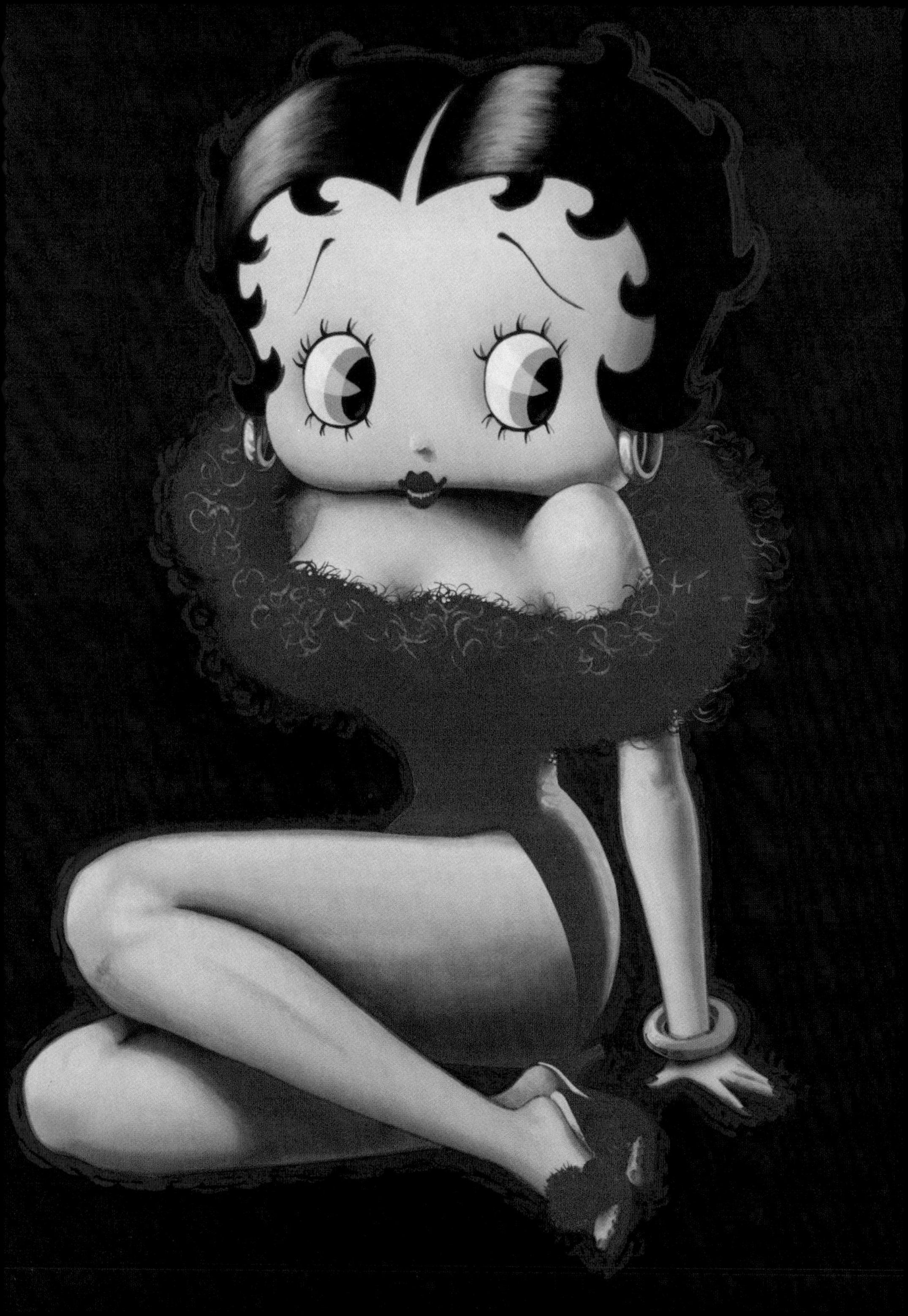

Introduction

Not many women have "it," but most every woman craves it . . . and I'm not talking about a heavy-duty trust fund or a high metabolism. Give up?

The X factor. That undeniable quality that more often than not proves to be the tipping point that gets you what you want. Existentially, literally, figuratively—you name it.

A woman with a quiet self-confidence, a smile that radiates, a healthy dose of sex appeal, and a sweetness all her own—that's the woman who will find true love, who can break any glass ceiling. She can manage her life, she will leave a lasting impression on whomever she connects with, and undoubtedly, she will inspire.

So, if age is just a number, and if my grandmother's sequined cashmere sweater is my most coveted fashion possession this season, then style is ageless. And Betty Boop, with X factor galore, has endless amounts to teach us about our own inner Boop!

For more than seventy years, Ms. Boop—as I so affectionately and

Betty Boop

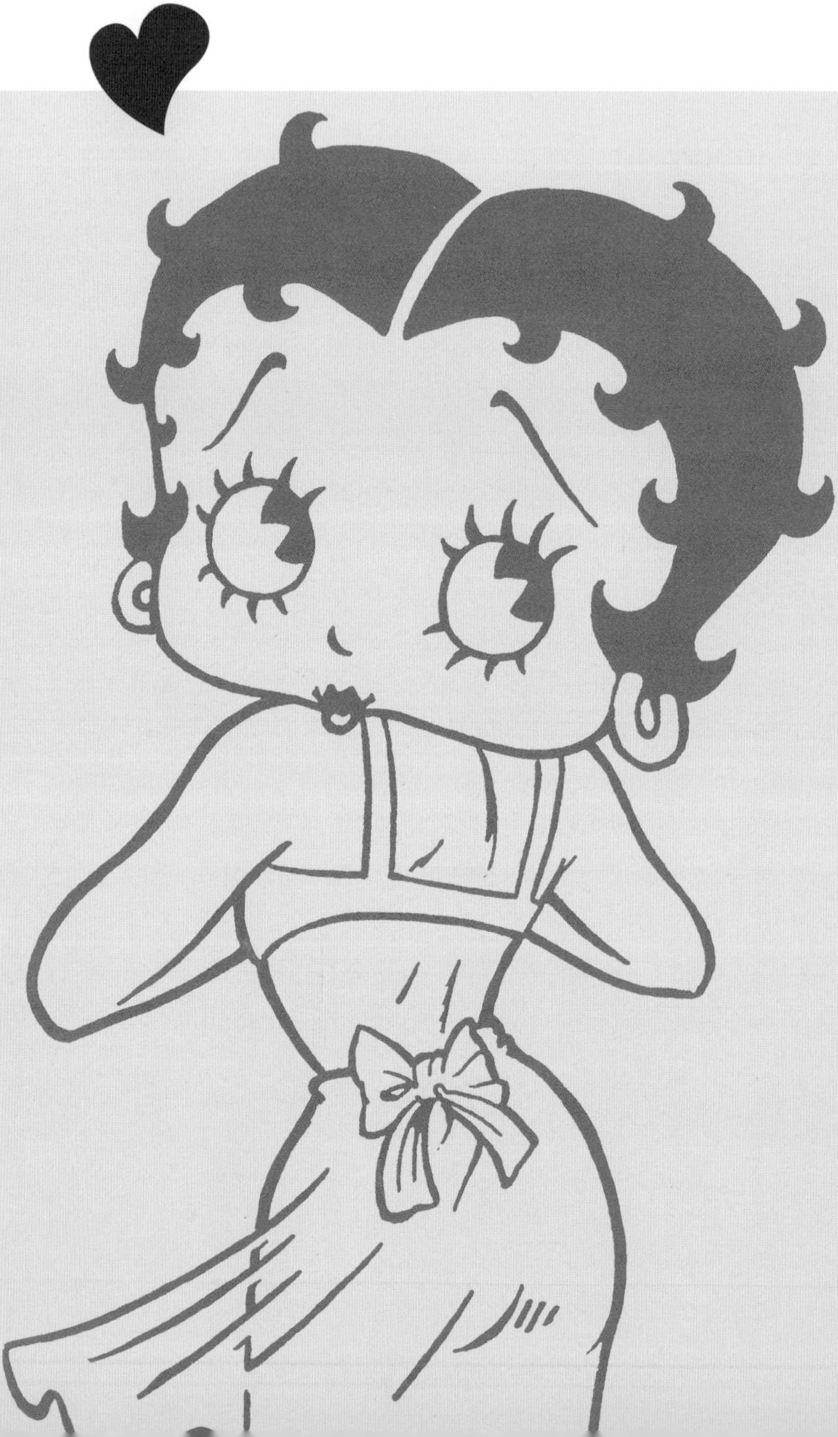

respectfully call her—has mesmerized millions. Men love her; girls adore her. I mean, how hard is that to pull off? Absolutely scrumptious, Betty's joie de vivre and sex appeal are the perfect recipe for lovable girlishness and fun! Her adventures, her trademark style, and her ability to handle any and every situation that's thrown her way make her an absolute original and a woman to watch, over and over again.

Beginning in 1930 (if you can even believe it), Betty set the stage and paved the way for strong, sexy full-figured women everywhere. Some of our biggest and brightest stars, icons of new and old, have been influenced by her universal appeal. From Marilyn Monroe to Madonna, there are traces of Betty everywhere.

What follows is a genuine Boop-a-fied road map to navigate you through anything and everything we modern gals have to master. So read on, and I promise that before you are through, you will know exactly how to be a Betty, too.

We all possess an inner Boop. All we need are the keys to release her!

Betty Boop

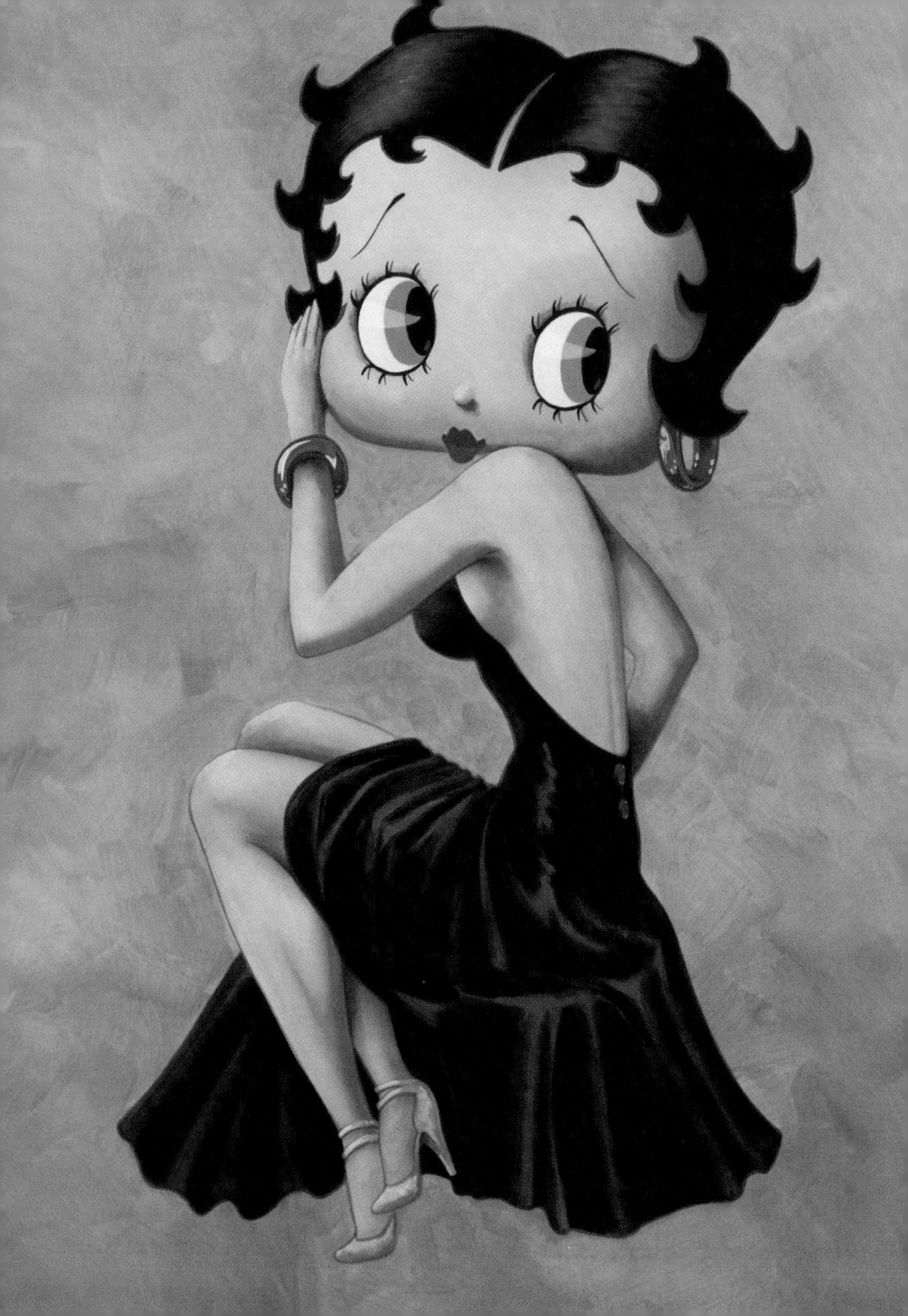

Chapter One

How to Glow Like Betty, and Then Some

Beauty, Diet, and General Health

To be beautiful on the outside, you first need to embrace your beauty on the inside, and no mere tip or trick can fix our state of minds! Our shells are genetically predetermined, so it's best to begin with inner work before you torture yourself with anything on the outside. With self-love and self-respect comes a radiance that only works to your advantage.

Obtaining that elusive self-acceptance is the absolute beginning of anything and everything that's beautiful. Loving thyself enables you to make great choices and gives you the courage and discipline to face daily obstacles. Whether they be quitting smoking, sticking to your diet, or setting aside time for yourself, your accomplishments will be limitless if you just love and respect yourself. So, take notice of the great person you are, and stop sizing yourself up in relation to others! Remember, with that love and respect, you may discover that your personal best is a size 12 and not a size 2.

Betty to the Rescue!

In today's world of endless beauty products and countless images of seemingly gorgeous women thrown our way, it's no wonder that many of us feel like we're on a high-speed roller coaster ride trying to determine which of the thousands of products, creams, masks, mists, and muds are right for us. It's dizzying, don't ya think? And incredibly expensive thank-you-very-much! Sometimes you have to think twice and wonder if we're all falling prey to a multi-million-dollar mega industry rather than reacting to an unexpected hormonal imbalance, a simple stress test, or perhaps a little too much butter on the popcorn we munched on during that late-night movie. But really, it's just so much simpler than the media, the beauty industry, or our own mind-sets would ever want us to believe. Okay, I'm not here to point fingers or state the obvious. Instead, I'm here to make developing your beauty regimen easy for you by sharing Betty's recipe for glowing, flowing beauty.

A life chock-full of Boop-oop-a-doop's starts right here!

Skin Deep—It All Starts Here

Sleep

Betty always made sure she got enough sleep to keep refreshed and upbeat throughout the day. A good night's sleep is an essential ingredient to glowing skin. (Nothing less than six hours a night.) Here's a secret weapon: Create your own sleep sanctuary! Allow me to explain.

Create an ambience once you shut your eyes that ensures plenty of restful z's. First, get your bed to feel as close to a fluffy cloud as possible. A yummy new goose down or Tempur-Pedic pillow, a mattress pad or feather bed, and maybe a lightweight down comforter . . . but that's just for starters. If your snuggle partner is out of town or out of the picture, not to worry; dust off your teddy bear, and hold him nice and tight. If that's too scary or too juvenile a concept, I totally understand. Because there's another solution: Go out and snatch up a body pillow. Give one a try, and you will never let anything or anyone come between the two of you. For real comfort mongers, there are also deluxe total-body maternity pillows. I'm serious.

Next, update your standard alarm clock with something special: a sound machine. There are plenty of clock radios that offer the natural sound effects that we all associate with wonderful soothing signs

Betty Boop

and magnificent memories like the ocean, a waterfall, the sound of summer nights, what have you. It's the best way to fall into a restful and plentiful sleep.

Then there's the idea of keeping a tidy space. I don't know about you, but when I finally get home from a long stressful day and my bedroom's a wreck, I just want to scream! Just think about how nice it is to walk into a bedroom that looks like a chambermaid had been there first. I'm not advocating crazy unrealistic neat freakishness, so don't go leaving yourself a gourmet chocolate on your pillow before you leave your house. Simply make your bed, catalog style, and put away the half-dozen outfits that you left all over the place when you tried to decide what to wear that day. That's all. It makes a big difference.

Additionally, get into the habit of spritzing your bedroom with a delicate fresh fragrance created especially for the home. Don't overdo it. It's best to keep this process to a minimum, maybe three to four times a week. Many of your favorite cosmetic and home decor companies have begun creating lovely scents specifically for this purpose. Choose a fragrance that you love—one that relaxes you and adds a sense of tranquillity, romance, and calm to your space. Popular favorites include lavender, cucumber, rose, vanilla, sake, ginger, and sugar.

Betty Boop

Some silent bells and whistles to consider to help you sleep long and lovely: When was the last time your bedroom saw a fresh coat of paint? One of the least expensive decorating remedies that offer some of the greatest rewards is just that—a paint job. Choose a soothing color that works well with the other staples in your space. Consider calming colors such as hues of light blues, shades of creams and caramels, or something suitable and charming in the lilac or rose families. Also, have you noticed that your bedroom receives a little too much light? Could that maybe have something to do with your lack of sleep? If so, invest in new shades, blinds, or drapes. Sheers may look gorgeous, but they could have a little something to do with those dark circles under your sleep-deprived eyes. And from a visual perspective, why not rid your room of some of the chaos and of those endless earned mementos. Fill it instead with a select few images that you admire, like a favorite print or a water-color. Also, a small grouping of treasured framed photographs on your night table is a great way to keep loved ones in your dreams.

Truly, if you rename and redesign your bedroom to become your sleep sanctuary, your skin will reap lasting effects, Betty style!

Betty Boop

Diet

More of the nice stuff and less of the naughty! Women who eat sensibly are more likely to enjoy a carefree complexion. It's a fact. And of course, yummy or not, fried foods are evil. Beyond making us gain weight, they wreak havoc on our skin. Indulge sometimes and celebrate when appropriate, but those three meals a day should include plenty of greens and proteins. Fresh fruits, nuts, seeds, beans, and vegetables are insanely beneficial to the skin and help reduce acne. Just remember, in the end, junk food doesn't taste as good as it looks and feels to have gorgeous, glowing skin.

Betty Boop

Soap and water are so underrated. And going to bed makeup free will do wonders! Starting your day after a morning cleansing ritual is a surefire home-grown spa treatment that will guarantee long-lasting aftereffects.

Mornings

Wake up with a warm-water rinse and a cleanser of your choice. Next apply a face moisturizer. A common mistake is using a *body* moisturizer, which naturally has a higher combination of oils and is often too rich for our pretty delicate faces. (A hand, foot, or body moisturizer on your face is an invitation to unwanted pimples and clogged pores!) Then apply your makeup, always remembering that "less is more."

Evenings

Before you repeat your warm-water rinse from your morning routine, first get specific with the makeup remover of your choice. Once makeup free, and depending upon the condition of your skin, choose an exfoliating or hydrating product to complete your mini midnight facial. Exfoliate and nourish your skin with a facial scrub product when you notice clogged pores and oil-based buildup, and use a hydrating polish when your face feels or seems dehydrated and dry.

Don't Bake

With the plethora of information out there about how detrimental the sun is to our skin, combined with all the great tinted moisturizers, bronzers, and now "spray tans" in the beauty aisle today, you'd have to be nuts to go out there without sun protection. Make sure you wear sunscreen when appropriate to avoid overexposure, and embrace your natural complexion as our beloved Ms. Boop does. Her porcelain skin is absolutely stunning and keeps her looking young and vibrant! Maintaining healthy skin, regardless of your natural born color, your ethnicity, or your exposure and proximity to the natural elements on the planet should be your top priority. Beyond making you look vibrant, a targeted skin regimen can stop Mother Nature in her tracks!

Being good to your skin is another wonderful way to maintain a glorious Betty glow.

Betty Boop

Makeup

Ms. Boop scores big in the beauty department! Have you ever seen such flawless makeup? Betty Boop knows what she needs, what works well for her, and what flows so seamlessly with the trends of our times, and so can you!

First, it's important to remember that the modern women we tend to emulate from a beauty perspective are all vamped out for magazine cover shoots, music videos, and ad campaigns—in addition, their images are *heavily* manipulated, smoothed, and "corrected" by the magazine designers. So, going to work, a wedding, or a first date is not the time to experiment with shocking makeup. And second, makeup artistry is in fact an art form, so if you don't expect to paint like Picasso, don't think you'll be able to smoke your own eyes like a professional makeup designer!

Skin

Now that you've been treating yourself to enough sleep, a healthy diet, a home facial regimen, and you have been protecting yourself from the sun, your skin should be at its finest! So, it's important not to take those few steps backward by caking your face with excess foundation and ruining all your progress. Let your skin breathe, and switch from those heavy foundations to a subtle tinted moisturizer. In addition, find two new blush shades that mirror your new healthy

Betty Boop

attitude and glow. I suggest a bronze shade and a rose one. A giant blush brush also ensures that your coverage spells perfection!

Eyes, Eyebrows, Shadows, and Mascara

They say that our eyes are the windows to our souls, so we all need to do what we can to brighten and accentuate them—appropriately. Take Betty, for example. Have you ever seen such gorgeous brows or a better use of mascara?

For your brows, find an eyebrow arching kit and get to work. You can find them everywhere these days, and when used correctly, they make such a difference! But please be careful. Overtweezing is the kiss of death, as is the wrong colored eyebrow pencil. Another solution, although a little more costly, is a monthly eyebrow wax. Be sure to bring along a photo as a visual reference of the shape you are looking for, just to make sure that you and the technician are on the same page. At the end of the day, well-kept eyebrows make a subtle yet very slick statement. Again, with shadow, less is more. A universal color palette that refreshes any skin type and works well day to evening, regardless of the activity or atmosphere, includes what I call "galaxy" tones, such as whites, creams, silvers, and golds.

Betty Boop

However, it's crucial that these colors are used ever so subtlely. They are meant to be applied just to the base of your eyelid and only as wide as your fingertip. That's it. A great waterproof mascara is key for any and every look. Thick luscious lashes set off everything else.

Lips

Here's where the fun starts! Matte for day and gloss for night. Choose your color based on occasion, what you're wearing, how you're feeling, and so forth. Find a signature color, if you so dare. (Betty's demure red pout is perfectly precious!) A sheer gloss over almost any color adds a richness and sometimes even deceives the eyes, appearing to enlarge the lips. (Faux collagen!) Just make sure your pearly whites stay clear of any color.

The idea is to shine. To glow. To be who you are and accentuate all your positives.

Betty Boop

Diet and Exercise—You're Not Built That Way!

Before J. Lo, there was Betty, so I say, "Long live our curves!"

An active healthy lifestyle is another key to Betty's undeniably rocking body. Betty's always up to something—always on the move, always on the go, all the while keeping up a social calendar that is filled to the brim. I can't quite imagine her in pajamas on her couch on a Friday night, diving headfirst into a pint of Ben & Jerry's. Can you? That's so not her style.

In the spirit of uncovering our inner Boop, it's time to motivate and get real when it comes to diet and exercise. Really, there's no way around it. Eat right and exercise. But as much as a healthy active lifestyle is about changing the way you live physically, (stairs versus elevators, workout versus TiVo marathons and shopping sprees), there is also a psychological and emotional metamorphosis that is so very essential. So, try not to look at a new gym membership as though it were a prison sentence, and at a side salad subbing for French fries as a punishment, but rather accept them as needed and welcomed major changes in your life. Developing a strong will is what will make you stick with it.

Betty Boop

Exercise

À la Betty, the key is to always be moving, thinking, learning, experimenting, meeting new people, trying new things . . . looking at your life as though it is an adventure—even if that means the hometown kind.

An active mind and an active life are the absolute staples in Betty's exercise routine.

Sweat, baby, sweat! Revving your heart rate and waking up your endorphins are essential in obtaining the body of your dreams! Thirty minutes of cardio five times per week may be unrealistic to maintain for the long haul, but for the first month it's the secret weapon for your body and your mind. And nothing feels better than the rush you get when you cool down. That sense of accomplishment will stick with you when temptations come a-knockin' and will also aid your body when it needs the extra energy to do whatever you've scheduled next at the gym (dance or step class, nautilus, free weights, and the like). Personally, I schedule cardio according to whatever reality show or red hot drama I'm obsessed with at the moment: I run on the treadmill while watching my favorite shows!

Betty Boop

Informal cardio is the king of exercise you can get in the "real world." This informal cardio is just as beneficial and a lot easier to squeeze into your day than strict visits to a gym. Some ideas . . .

- Stroller derby! Meet other new moms at the local park, at the beginning of your neighborhood block, or even at your favorite indoor shopping mall. By incorporating toddler time into your exercise program and social schedule, you benefit from every angle! Make sure to wear the correct foot gear and keep a step counter attached to your waistline. Be on the safe side, and leave your credit cards at home.

- Get outside and make workouts a family affair. Get your loved ones to help motivate you, and allocate a weekly weekend afternoon that you can spend quality time together while getting your heart rates up. Drag your husband away from one of the ten ball games he juggles on the weekend, and see if he can keep up with you at the nearest track.

- Gas gauge! Consider where and how often you are in your car, and then reconsider what small journeys and errands can be done without the horsepower. If your local library, video store, or beauty salon is within walking distance, why not do just that and walk or jog to and fro? And for you city dwellers, if you live on an upper floor, save energy and get in a little stair climbing.
- Pet friendly. Woman's best friend can now also be her personal trainer. Take your pampered pooch with you on your next long-distance walk. Enjoy the companionship, the security, and the entertainment value—pass the time, and press the pavement with a brisk walk and a select number of sprints, and you both will reap the rewards.
- Create an abbreviated home gym by purchasing several items that can help you work out and burn calories in the comforts of your own home. If you have the means and the space, a tread-mill placed specifically near a window or in close proximity to your television (and not far from your favorite Betty Boop poster) is ideal. Medicine balls, jump ropes, a free-weight set, a yoga mat, and a variety of excellent and highly consumer-recommended exercise tapes like yoga, Pilates, step aerobics, and so on, are also great ways to get you moving and grooving in the privacy, comfort, and convenience of your own home.

The gym is a great place to get your glam on. A gym membership, if possible, is worth it. Then there are no excuses!

What to look for when joining a gym:

- Proximity. Find a gym that is no more than twenty minutes from your home, so the effort of getting there is never an excuse to stay home.
- Affordability. Find a gym that you can afford, so that money is never an issue.
- Join a coed gym. Eye candy will sweeten the experience and likely make those thirty minutes on the treadmill fly by just as quickly as watching music videos could. Also, perhaps a certain someone will help motivate you to work a little harder, jog a little longer, whatever it takes.
- Classes. Mix it up! Having the option to try the latest and greatest new classes will only enhance your workout and keep your interest and enjoyment high!
- Bells and whistles. Salon, spa, snack bar, on-site trainers, top-notch facilities—any of these will make working out convenient, enjoyable, and interesting!

Once you've dropped those first few pounds, the gratification of a flatter tummy or better-fitting jeans will keep you amped and proud,

Betty Boop

and it will make saying no to seconds (and thirds!) a lot easier. Best of all, dieting will then feel like a special personal challenge that you'll want to accomplish! (Healthy you versus unhealthy you.) Just stick with it and don't give up. The easy way never does pan out, you know. Unfortunate, but oh so true!

Diet

Betty managed to maintain her great weight and great shape long before the fat-free craze came and went and before any man, woman, or child had even heard of the Atkins diet.

Come on, now, you know you know better!

Let's be honest: Listen to your body. If you're full, you're full. If you feel gluttonous, stop dead in your tracks and buy, order, or dine on something different, something better for you.

1. Don't skip breakfast. A bowl of oat bran, some fruit, an egg, or maybe Egg Beaters.
2. Lunch. A great big yummy salad with all your favorite veggies, grilled chicken or salmon, and a light dressing of your choice. (Always ask for "light" and "on the side.")
3. Din din. Before seven p.m., make sure you've got three food groups represented here. A nice piece of meat, fish, or poultry.

Betty Boop

Grilled, seasoned, and so forth. A small side of veggies and a tiny bit of bread. Brown rice instead of white. Pita rather than buttered rolls or bread sticks, some noodles, perhaps.

It's not just the big three that are important. Keep the following in mind:

- Water. Six to eight glasses of water each day will fill you up, clean you out, and will help curb your appetite.
- Snacks and dessert. Give yourself a break each day. Something small and something sensible. Light, unbuttered, unsalted popcorn; licorice sticks; a fistful of almonds; low-fat yogurt or ice cream.
- And for you caffeine addicts, whether it's one or four cups a day, you've got to introduce skim milk into your life. Try subbing those sugar packets for a suitable sugar substitute, and if at all possible, change to decaf every now and again. And as for those highly decorated coffee drinks—the mocha, frappé, and cappuccinos—the calorie counts are endless! Small changes reap big rewards.

The key with your diet is this: If you eat right and you maintain your cardio and workout regimen, the body you were born to have will materialize over time. It's a fact. Have patience and willpower, and all good things will come.

Betty Boop

Here are a few noncaloric helpful hints to presenting a slimmer and healthier you:

- Possessing great posture makes you appear longer and leaner and conveys a strong sense of self. Yoga and Pilates are two secret weapons.
- Footwear with pointed toes rather than round can fool the eye and make you appear taller and longer.
- Cap-sleeved tops that bare a bit of your shoulder set off your regal stature.
- Faux slenderizing is now all too possible, all too comfortable, and very beneficial. You can "lose" five pounds instantly by wearing several of the latest and greatest support-based designs. Lingerie stores carry up-to-the-minute modernized undergarments that do the job and don't leave you feeling caged or suffocated.
- Add inches! Like it or not, your pumps and high heels make you sleek like nobody's business. If that's an uncomfortable option, get yourself a pair of kitten heels. They give you an added inch. And as the saying goes, every inch counts. Betty's shoe collection is piled up with any and every high-heel option.
- And finally, dark solid colors. Blacks and blues slim and trim in ways that pastels and prints don't.

The Fine Art of Fashion—Keep in Style

When you look good, you feel good, and your inner Boop will shine through.

One of the best things about being a woman in today's world is the access we have to expressing our personal style. With shopping malls, factory outlets, e-commerce fashion sites, boutiques, novelty shops, and resale stores at our fingertips, every kind of garment is at our disposal, at every price point and for every occasion. We have magazines, television, new and old films, literature, art—you name it. If there's a look out there that suits us, that inspires us, it is often just an arm's length away.

So with the abundance of clothing and style options, we need to determine what exactly is right for us, both generally and specifically. And when I say *right*, I mean, appropriate, flattering, and, most important, realistic.

Fashion Keys

Being a fashion chameleon can get expensive, chaotic, a wee bit confusing to our friends and family, and really, who has the closet space? So, determining *personal style* should be your fashion priority.

Prior to shopping and dressing, you need to determine the overall look that you are going for: comfortable casual, sexy, trendy, classic, sophisticated, mod, urban, rocker, punk, preppy, or boho, for example. When pondering all of this, think about your lifestyle—consider your interests, age, and your environment. And most of all, determine what you are most comfortable projecting. Looking to a fashion icon for inspiration is a great way to get started. From our dear Ms. Betty Boop to Audrey Hepburn and Marilyn Monroe. Your favorite musicians, a Gwen Stefani, a Carly Simon, a Faith Hill. Supermodels like Kate Moss and Tyra Banks or power women like Oprah Winfrey and Diane Sawyer. These women have each cultivated a consistent look over time, and as their fashion choices progress, their personal style never wavers.

Once you've decided on your personal style, you need to realize that Rome wasn't built in a day. Make sure that you have a handful of key pieces at your disposal; then you can make them work with what's currently hanging in your closet and folded in your drawers!

Betty Boop

Key pieces should be thought of as the quintessential garments that you would associate with the overall style you are trying to achieve.

- [ ] **The *essential* jacket or blazer.** If you were going for a "mod" look, you would find a great trim-fitting short black blazer.
- [ ] **The *model* jean or casual pant.** If you were going for a "sophisticated" look, you would want to have a pair of chino trousers or clam diggers.
- [ ] **The *standard* dress or evening piece.** If you were thinking "classic," you would find a great black knee-length cocktail dress.
- [ ] **The *versatile* boot, pump, sneaker, or slipper.** If you were feeling the "sexy" thing, you would choose a black patent leather high-heel shoe.
- [ ] **The *archetypal* top.** If you were going for a "trendy" look, then a sequined short-sleeve blouse would be perfect.
- [ ] **The *classic* bag.** If "boho" is your thing, you'd search high and low for an oversize shoulder slouch bag.
- [ ] **The *typical* accessory: jewelry, cap or hat, belt, or scarf.** If you were eyeing a "preppy" look, you would choose a pearl necklace.

Now, before you go shopping or get set to get dressed, you need to also be aware of your body type and the selection of silhouettes that are most flattering on you. Be as aware of your positives as you are of

Betty Boop

your negatives. Work all the angles. So, if your waistline, shoulders, or legs are your most coveted attributes, accentuate them by choosing pieces that will showcase them. Likewise, if you are not comfortable with your stomach area or you've got this thing with your arms, work with pieces that camouflage and conceal.

Betty, for instance, works her curves magically. She draws attention to her small waistline by wearing more fitted looks. She tones her curves perfectly with solid colors, and she flaunts her great legs by paying close attention to hemlines and by always rocking a sexy set of heels. A true style master!

Furthermore, colors, patterns, and prints can do wonders when we choose the right ones. Much like when we're decorating, we need to be very conscious of what works with what and which colors, patterns, and prints do us the most justice.

Here are some related fashion factoids to pay attention to:

- While solids and darker colors conceal and draw the eyes else-where, dots and prints—although tons of fun—tend to have the opposite effect. So, be careful where you sport the sizzle and the shine.
- Stripes have earned a reputation for the consistent addition of width and volume; therefore don them according to your unique shape.
- Beware that lighter colors are inclined to be as honest as possible.
- Patterns and prints tend to make grand statements and often lose their versatility and wearability much too soon. So when thinking dollars and cents, make the larger investment in a piece or pieces that are more key.

There's nothing more girly and fun than accessories, but they can still be dangerous to your wardrobe if you get it wrong. Best put, accessories should be kept to a minimum. Overaccessorizing can stomp out a perfectly great look. Your bag, your shoes—those are your staples. The jewelry, the scarves, the belts, and the hats—simply gravy. So, when you are just about to accessorize, take inventory. Look in the mirror, and if your outfit seems near perfect, choose something demure, like a great pair of earrings or a lovely long necklace. Conversely, if the image before you seems flat, incorporate that smart hat or beautiful belt.

Lastly, your pocketbook need not suffer during your style transformation. In a blink of an eye, high fashion gets translated to every income level. Use photos from your favorite magazines as inspiration and then be your own fashion editor, shopping until you find "it"—the more reasonable version of what you are coveting. Also, get creative by bartering with friends and family. Lending or trading different pieces keeps your look fresh and never boring. Be clever by rotating your wardrobe to appear endless and right on! And then there are the factory outlets, eBay, and flea markets: a fashionista's very best friends.

The main thing is this: You don't have to spend gobs of cash to look like you do. And you don't need to be a trendsetter or a style innovator. The crucial aspect, above all else, is to have a strong sense of pride and a great sense of self. It's not about the size of your jeans but, more important, about picking the best jeans for you—the ones that will make you feel and look your best. With a strong sense of self comes a captivating aura and a positive attitude. Just like the woman we are honoring throughout these pages, Ms. Betty Boop. Understanding what to wear and how to wear it will only compliment and further bring out the very best aspects of you.

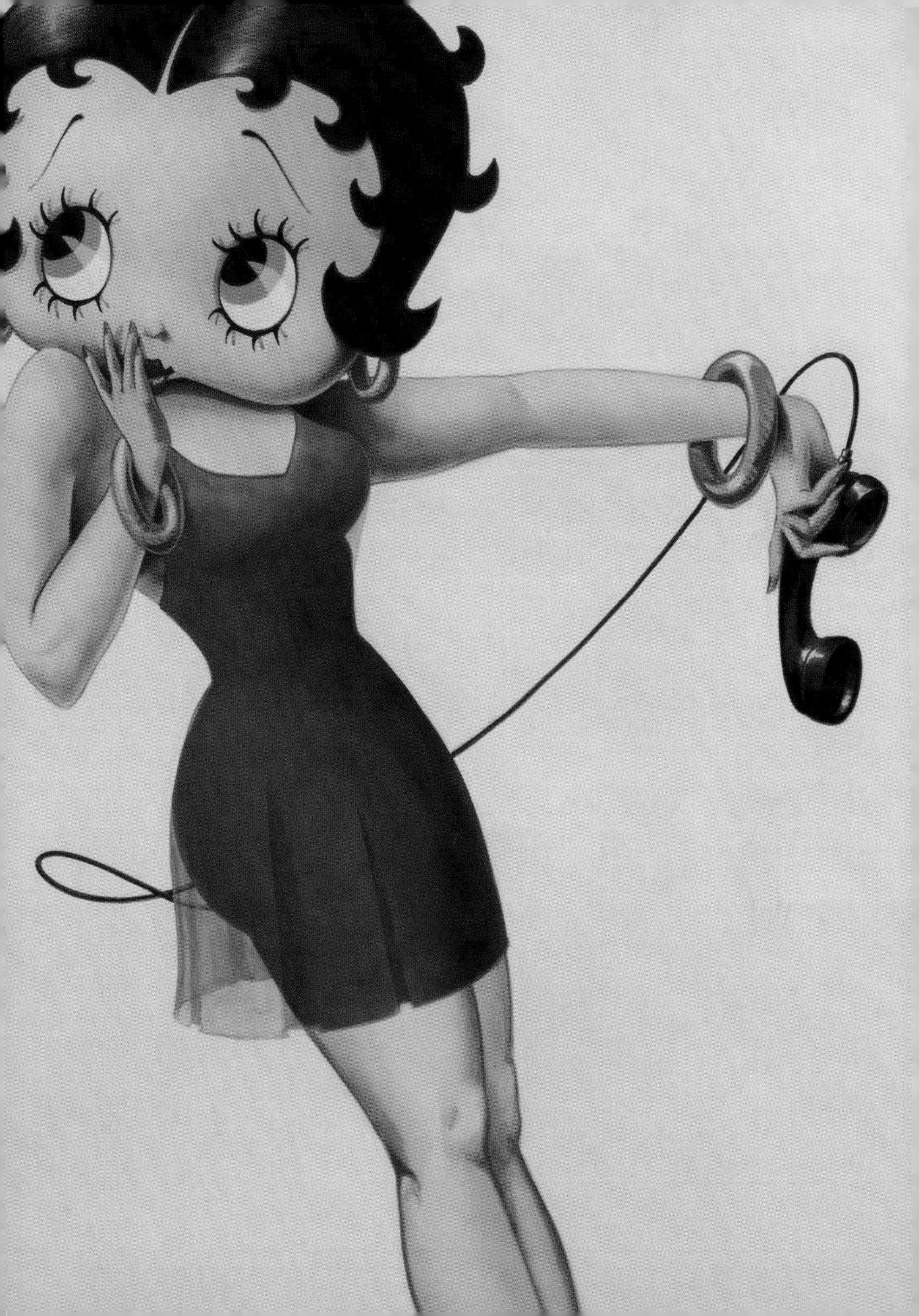

Chapter Two

How to Be a Betty At Work

The Business of Business, Betty Style

If there were ever a recipe to achieving success in our chosen career paths, it would surely include three key ingredients. The formula would no doubt call for one part timing, one part luck, and one part mastery!

Timing and luck have an influence in the life of a successful career woman. Being in the right place at the right time. These elements are, as far as I know, completely out of our control. However, the third ingredient—mastery in one's field and of one's actions in that field—is absolutely fundamental, totally attainable, and the golden ticket to your eventual success.

The good news is that there is indeed a master blueprint that can guide you toward ascension and success. Mastery is about possessing a game plan, a design, a method, and it enables you to have a better sense of confidence and control. The bad news—it takes a great deal of hard work, focus, and huge amounts of patience and dedication, all the while holding a pleasant, optimistic outlook.

Ms. Boop's Master Blueprint

Follow the Yellow Brick Road

Had Dorothy never followed that great advice, she would definitely never have reached Oz or met up with that wizard! For you, the key is to determine your goal, carve out a plan, and follow it. When making this decision, you should be as close to certain as possible that your industry of choice is the right one for you. Think bigger at first, rather than focusing on a specific job or position. Getting started, no one ever thoroughly understands the dynamics and structure of the business they want to get into. Thinking a bit more generally early on gives you room to breathe and grow should your desires, interests, and circumstances change along the way. When determining your career goals, please make sure that your field is one that will hold your interest and keep you passionate over time. Five days a week, typically ten to twelve hours of each day, for what will feel like an eternity after a short while—you really better love what you do!

Mark a Mentor

Once you've scored a coveted position and you've comfortably become acquainted with the way things work within your department and your company, you'll undoubtedly gain exposure to a select few individuals who shine and are a bit further along than yourself. He or she, for whatever the reasons (and I'm sure there'll be many), has gotten that far by enduring a learning curve with many ups, downs, and bumps along the way. Needless to say, there's a lot you can learn from these individuals. And oftentimes, they are more than happy to share their own invaluable experiences and advice with someone who genuinely admires their tactics, their energy, and their success. Mark this individual, your mentor, and your relationship. The benefits will be endless.

Know Thyself

By acknowledging your strengths and weaknesses, you are likely to increase your chances of success, both in the present and the future. Stand-out team players are the perfect examples. They delegate properly and efficiently, they take on tasks and challenges where the percentage ratio of failure is slim to none, they ask for assistance when appropriate, and they shine when they execute with efficiency and ease. If you have questions, ask them. If you need extra time, request it, rather than delivering late. And if you possess expertise in a given scenario, offer it. Knowing thyself is the way to go.

Become a Guru

Know your industry inside and out. In a world of such fierce competition, you only increase your likelihood of success by doing your homework. Subscribe to the appropriate trade journals, and keep tabs on what's happening in the business world around you. Work to possess a wide understanding about your product, your competition, the marketplace, the innovators, the troublemakers, and so on. If it means a little extra time, effort, and energy, it will be worth it to you down the road.

Keep Up with the Joneses

Brush up on your skills and keep up with technology. Be as proficient as possible and watch as your value within your organization rises. In this day and age, if you want to get ahead, it's not enough to be the average. You want to be the go-to girl. And she is as much of a teacher and problem solver as she is a cog in the wheel. Trust me.

Be a Social Butterfly

Network like mad. The best way to build first-class relationships is to get out from behind your desk and get out there, into the real world, for more face time and human interaction. Socializing builds on relationships with colleagues, clients, vendors, and potential partners in a way that typical and standard corporate communications never will and never can. In addition, networking can also be your own version of a passive public relations or recruitment campaign on your very own behalf. Let the competition know you exist and see you in action. Don't wait for a search firm to find you a better job or a more lucrative opportunity. Make it happen for yourself.

Amen

Practice what you preach! Ideally, you should be passionate about your corporate culture. Believing in your product, in the corporate philosophies, mantras, and the like only makes your job, your day, your week, your year that much more pure, that much more easy, and that much more pleasant not only for you but for all those you come in contact with.

Take It Easy

Sometimes success can be measured not only by achievement, contribution, and commitment, but also by winning that under-the-radar yet still very real office popularity contest. Betty Boop wins this prize time and time again. After careful observation, it is clear that those who are easygoing, easy to work with, and easy to please, nine times out of ten, get the furthest. Sure, there will always be that one individual whose success is utterly perplexing, but let's just chalk that phenomenon up as one of life's great mysteries. In most cases, temperamental, hot-under-the-collar, grumpy types tend to be overlooked when scarce growth opportunities, raises, and bonuses arise. Your goal should always be to be perceived as the ideal candidate, the most deserving, the one. So, always think twice before speaking up and speaking out. Basically, pick your battles, and attempt to kill even the worst of colleagues or supervisors with kindness. You've got to grin and bear it when that's a viable option. Business is a lot like politics. Not only do you need to be good at what you do, but you need to be equally skilled at dealing with people and taking the high road. So, take it easy, try to be positive, and think before you act.

Image Maker

To be taken seriously in the business world, you need to look serious. Thankfully, nowadays, "serious," as in business attire, cannot be so easily or so readily defined. What started out as casual Fridays circa 1996-ish—well, that mind-set has slowly infiltrated our Mondays, Tuesdays, Wednesdays, and Thursdays. (Hip, hip hooray!) So, today, personal style and personal expression, the desire to convey our own uniqueness and individuality in the workplace, are widely and practically universally accepted. Lucky us!

Betty Boop

What to Wear? What to Wear?

Consider the following prior to dressing for work.

First Impressions

Being feminine and sexy is completely acceptable, but of course, there's a limit. Calling attention—and I mean tons of attention—to your most favorite body part is not exactly the sign of profound professionalism. They say that you never get a second chance to make a first impression, so why muck it up with a whole lotta you so early in the a.m.? Keep the cleavage to a minimum. Save the belly shirts for nighttime, and please, oh please, leave your low-low-low-rise bottoms for the bars! Your goal is to gain the respect from both your male and female counterparts, and not to alienate and offend them. Yeesh! (Also worth mentioning: the manicure. If you tend to gnaw under pressure, stop. If that's not a possibility, keep a standing weekly manicure appointment. The best ten bucks you'll ever spend!)

Environment

Of course, if you work at a record label, the dress code is going to be much more lax than shall we say, the public defender's office, so bend any of the following suggestions where applicable.

Betty Boop

Comfort and Function

What looks hot may not feel hot when push comes to shove. Case in point: vicious, jaw-dropping, high, heavenly heels. If and when the fashionista in you persists, and a great pair of black strappies just so makes your outfit du jour, go crazy and rock 'em. However, play it smart by keeping a pair of suitable standards in your desk's bottom drawer, just in case. And how about that lovely, crisp, white-hot button-down that, although a little snug, does wonders for your bust and waistline? Think twice with a darling camisole underneath to protect against the unexpected yet all-too-common peep show. You know where I'm going with this, right? When your middle to top button, worn from the wear and tear of one too many visits to the dry cleaners, decides to pop or break off—or heaven forbid, opts to unbutton itself without your prior knowledge or permission—it's the kind of

Betty Boop

embarrassment one should avoid if humanly possible. Then there's that too-tight but oh-so-slimming pencil skirt. If you love the silhouette but hate how constricted it makes you feel, shop for garments that incorporate Lycra and possess miraculous stretching powers. The stretch factor is almost a given in most cottons, denims, and wool these days, so not to worry, you'll have plenty of options. Also, avoid linens at all costs. Although intensely comfortable, they wrinkle at the drop of a hat. From bottoms to tops, I say make linen a weekend ritual.

When My Ship Comes In . . .

Right about now, you've got your career goals and plans in order. You're dressed to impress and ready for success. You're kicking serious butt at the office, and even better, you've managed to change your personal lifestyle. You're sleeping better, eating healthier, are busy as a bee, energized, and feeling fit, strong, and healthy. Your friends have told you that you've never looked better, and now you're ready, willing, and highly deserving of a much-needed raise. Still, the burning question in fact burns: How do I go about getting it? Not to worry, Betty and I have cooked up a logical plan to help you go in there and get one!

Assess

When asking for a raise, you need to be prepared for any reactions. Therefore, the case you make for yourself needs to be foolproof. Not to worry, here's a quick checklist to review:

- [ ] You have been in the position for at least one full year.
- [ ] You have reached and in most cases surpassed the goals and responsibilities allocated to you from day one.
- [ ] You have not experienced any problems with attendance or tardiness.
- [ ] You are prepared to handle an increased workload, additional responsibilities, oversee additional staff, or spend a greater number of days on the road or in the office, as such demands may be required of you with a salary increase. (This is something to truly consider. If your raise is contingent on many if not all of the above, you need to determine whether you really are ready for "more" and if the proposed new salary is a fair and balanced one.)
- [ ] You are a team player.
- [ ] Your enthusiasm and work ethic inspire others.
- [ ] You have thought about ways in which you can improve your company's spending, morale, productivity, and so forth.
- [ ] You envision yourself at this company for an extended amount of time and are you committed to your job and to your company.

Betty Boop

☐ You are prepared to make a change should your superior or company not recognize your commitment and achievements or match them with a financial commitment of their own. (That's a tough one, but still this is something you need to think about should you not get the response you are hoping for.)

Plan Ahead

Before engaging in the "I want a raise" conversation with your supervisor, it's best to create a new job description: one that reflects what you honestly feel is the natural progression for you within your department or company. This description should represent your expected growth, the addition of responsibilities, increased management involvement—compensating and validating an adjusted salary and title if all goes well. It will not only convey your professionalism and enthusiasm, but it will also serve as a fantastic mental and organizational exercise for your peace of mind. The preparation that goes into this task will make for great talking points during your upcoming meeting. I also suggest that you discuss your expectations with your mentor or, at the very least, with a trusted confidant, as it is always good to hear a second and more unbiased point of view prior to such a big moment in your professional journey.

Good luck!

Service with a Smile

Despite all your efforts, the business world can eat you alive if it's hungry enough. If you're not prepared for those touchy subjects, ones even the aces of aces have experienced, well, you're doomed for heartache. So here's a cheat sheet should any drama come your way.

Coworker Confrontations

Ugh. Just when you thought you left the sandbox and the playground way back in elementary school, sometimes even consenting adults just won't play nice. Your best bet here is to employ whatever methods necessary not to lose your cool! Besides practicing yoga and meditation in your off time, or biting your likely already all-too-sore tongue, you need to get into the practice of waiting till all the smoke has cleared before you even respond. Taking the time to get into a rational frame of mind should be your number one priority. Second on your list is to move the party into a private or concealed space. Being the topic of office banter is not what you've worked this hard for. Always being polite, even with someone who likely doesn't deserve it, will aid in your mission to speak nonregrettably and completely clearly. You also want to try to be the peacekeeper in the scenario so that you will, no matter what, always end up on top. Do whatever it takes to squelch the situation so that your superiors need not get involved, and finally, if the matter does worsen, schedule a personal meeting with your human resources representative or adviser. Taking the high road, tracking your efforts, and handling the unfortunate situation with grace and professionalism are the best ways to deal with coworker confrontations.

Slave Labor

For a while, it may be a means to earning your stripes, paying your dues, or covering your back—however, when you begin to feel like the job you signed up for is not the job you are doing, at some point you are going to need to raise a white flag and attempt to rectify the situation.

First of all, you need to take a good look at your own organizational skills, the ways in which you prioritize, and the manner in which you delegate responsibility within your organization or your department. Ask yourself if it is at all possible that should you make some changes to your normal methods and routines, the problems you are having in this area might be straightened out, prior to registering a complaint or giving up.

Betty Boop

Some helpful hints:

- Get to work an hour earlier than the norm. Use the quiet and calm to your advantage. Get the tedious and the frivolous out of the way, as another hectic day surely awaits you. One early hour can save you from several late ones.
- Get in the habit of making lists, and prioritize each item. Although every day will bring new surprises, interruptions, and tasks, by keeping a running list, your odds of falling off track are minimized.
- Acquire a practice of not making or taking personal calls at the office. By training your friends and family to respect your work time, you will automatically buy yourself extra hours every week. Keep the phone lines open to emergencies, and learn to love instant messaging instead.

Should the problem persist, and you're sure it's not about you or your abilities, schedule time with your manager or direct supervisor and discuss the matter through. On the bright side, the chances are strong that your issues can be easily remedied. Maybe a new assistant will do the trick or an updated computer program or a promotion for someone on your team who can pick up some of the slack. Or maybe it's just about making some-one else aware of the situation, and then they, too, will change the way they operate and leave you to do your thing, the right way. Betty and I will cross our fingers in your behalf!

Several more scribbles while we're still on the topic of "touchy subjects" to be conscious of:

- Keep a paper trail of all important communications, just to be on the safe side.
- Don't mix business with pleasure. In most cases, the negatives outweigh the positives.
- Don't make promises you can't keep to your support staff, to your superiors, or to your clients.
- Always remember that your online communications with family, friends, and otherwise may be monitored.
- Despite what we'd all love to be the case, an expense account is not a personal one.

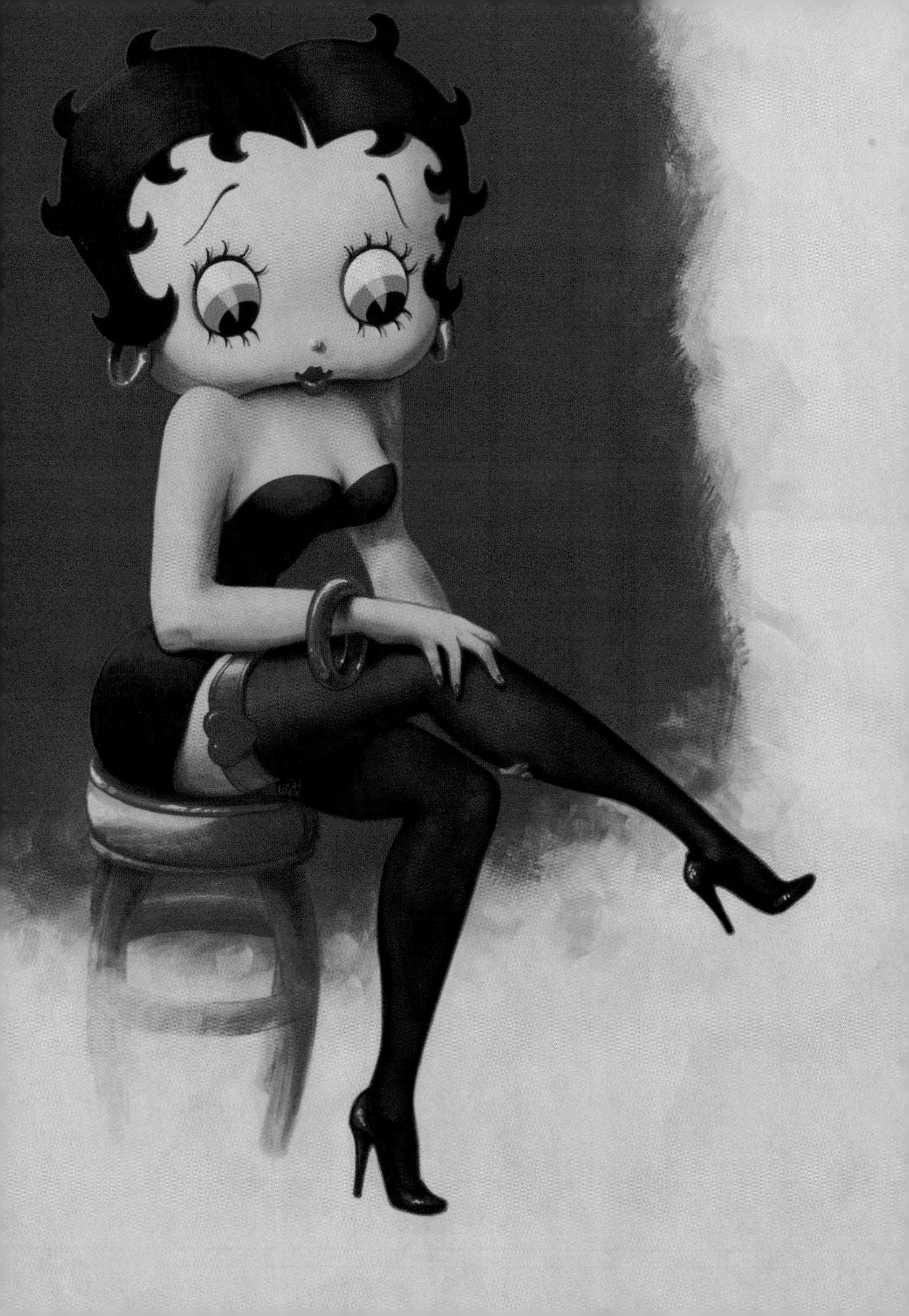

Chapter Three

How to Be a Betty in Love

Dating, Spouses, Singledom

We all start out single, we begin dating, and we may make a commitment to one person. If all goes well, there's possibly marriage and then, well, the whole happily-ever-after thing.

Wouldn't life be grand if it were only that simple!

Singledom and Dating

As far as love and relationships go, none of us can make the right decision about a prospective partner until we've spent some quality time with ourselves. This should be a scientific fact of life, if it isn't already. But alas, many of us frantically fear the idea of being alone—in the same way we fear skydiving or air turbulence, or not getting an Evite to an incredible shoe sale. And that really is an unfortunate thing. Fear invites poor decisions of the impulsive, neurotic, and subconscious kind. A little alone time is simply that—a little

moment in time, not the eventual state of our entire lives, and forgetting that breeds trouble of the romantic kind, for sure!

So I say, and Ms. Boop totally agrees, embrace your singledom! Own it, love it, and you'll soon see that the right person will appear when the time—key word here—is just *right*!

Benefits: Mind, Body, and Soul

In the right frame of mind, being single is a blessing in disguise. You finally have the time to get to know yourself: who you really are, what you are really about, what you really need, and what you truly are looking for in life. Your confidence builds, your independence grows, and there are no more excuses. You hit the gym, you get through that giant novel, you spend quality time with friends and family. Finally, you travel, you climb the corporate ladder, and you try new things. You enjoy all the fruits of your labors, and it's so about time! Once fear and desperation are long gone, positive, healthy decision making—when it comes to opportunities and events of the single kind—all seem to flow.

- You say yes more. You're open to new things and new experiences, whether it's a blind date or a night out on the town, and so forth. Suddenly, what used to feel safe and comfortable, like a Friday night at Blockbuster, now seems way lame and a poor excuse for an evening.

- You take risks, taking the first step. Maybe you chat up someone who meets your fancy. Or you finally cave and go out with the person your mother, boss, dentist has been dying to set you up with—because now you possess an open mind.
- You start expanding your social circle. The freshness of your life draws in new and interesting people and situations. You may even start dating someone who you would once have cast off as "not your type" or "just-friends material."
- You don't sweat it when you don't get a call, e-mail, or text message immediately. You're in a great healthy state of mind. If you know the date went well, you can wrap your brain and your heart around the notion that you most definitely will be contacted.
- And most of all, you no longer convince yourself that some guy is all that and a big bowl of Doritos. You don't fret and freak out if you get an "I'm just not that into you," because as silly and corny as it may sound, you love yourself, and if that person doesn't get it, well, your sense of self is solid as a rock. And although you may be mildly insulted and slightly bummed out (and rightly so, by the way, because you are a human being), still, you will know in your heart of hearts that the idea and energy spent trying to make someone fall for you are just so not worth it and so not what you are about anymore.

Take our adorable Betty. Imagine if she settled for the wrong man? Where would her adventures be? Her sexy devilish spirit? Her delicious laugh? Her beautiful smile? See what I mean? Chalk it up to that Boop factor!

Let Me Call You Sweetheart

After a little practice, dating is just like riding a bike, driving a car, curling our eyelashes. The mystery, the fear factor, figuring it all out and playing the game, gets easy and, even better, feels comfortable in time. And the great thing is, once you unlock, unleash, and harness that X factor—or better put, your Boop factor—it all appears, and really feels, absolutely natural.

Prioritize

To begin with, figure out all the qualities in a person that are *important* to you versus *essential* for you, because there's a very big difference. And there is also reality. Whatever molecular miracles were involved in the making of Brad Pitt will likely never happen again in our lifetime. Seriously, while I'm not advocating the idea of settling, everyone needs to realize that no one is perfect. That no one is or will ever be perfect, but rather, that out there, somewhere, is the perfect person for you. To make this distinction is the first step to clarity of the romantic kind. And then, once your heart and your mind are communicating effectively, when you've encountered a serious candidate or conversely when you haven't hit the mark exactly, you'll be equipped psychologically and emotionally to know exactly how to handle it. Better still, by prioritizing, you'll know fairly soon during the dating process if and when your date isn't right for you. So, rather than a slow dive, you'll come to a resolution in good time and you'll feel very good about your choices. And more important, you'll have increased your odds of running into or meeting your Prince Charming all the more swiftly.

Protocol

Be mysterious! Nine men out of ten will tell you that there is something fascinating and majorly alluring about a woman who does not drop everything and everyone for a guy she's just met. A woman who plays it close to the vest and eventually and reasonably allows a courtship to grow into a relationship is making all the right choices and is so much more attractive to the man that she desires.

Cheat Sheet

1. Save the drama for your mama—or, of course, your very best friends.

First dates are not the time to unload your frustrations, insecurities, or lackluster attributes (that is, credit-card debt or your ingrown hair trauma). Show the best version of you. Your interests, passions, priorities. When we talk about what we love and what we enjoy, we shine, and that's what you want the guy across from you or next to you to see.

2. Let them talk.

You want to end date one with a good sense of who this person is and what they are all about. Ask questions and listen. You'll learn a lot, and you'll have the right tools to determine if there should be a date two.

3. Order what you want.

Don't become yet another tragic woman who seems to eat like a little-bitty butterfly on a first date. (And please don't order the most expensive dish on the menu. Lots of men notice and dislike that!)

4. Drink sensibly.

Nervous or not, don't drink to feel calm. You and I both know what can happen there. Besides blurting out that you haven't been kissed in what feels like a decade or how your ex left you at the altar, you don't want to end the date not knowing or remembering exactly what you talked about, and even worse, you don't want your first evening together to turn into a first morning all at once!

Betty Boop

5. Be the girl your parents would be proud of.

For as long as humanly possible, at any rate! Love at first sight is a definite possibility, but there is no woman out there who can honestly say that she really knew what the guy was about, where he'd "been," and what he was made of after a great first date. If you're worried about regrets, let's not make sleeping with him after four hours one of them. I'm a huge advocate of a long first kiss (they're the best), but take whatever measures possible to leave Lance Romance streetside when you come home. Besides making your folks proud, you will feel a thousand times better in the morning, and undoubtedly you will have left him wanting more. Tons more!

6. When he calls . . .

Do not call, text, or e-mail him first. Call it customary, chivalrous, or call me jaded, I don't care: Just let him call you first. And if by chance you miss his call, let him sweat it out a bit. Maybe an hour or a day even. (It will be our little secret.)

7. Get-togethers and hangouts.

That's guy speak for "booty call." You've got to wait a bit, a few more dates, before you accept that kind of invitation. As sweet and innocent as it may seem or that the invite may in fact be, after a few glasses of wine, your strength and suffocated morality will be thoroughly tested.

8. Friends with families and family gatherings.

Major no-no's in the beginning. Get this new guy in a room with all

Betty Boop

your coupled-off friends and their kids or Mom and Dad and your grandma, and he's likely going to feel a wee bit of pressure, legitimate or not. Keep your courtship private, light, and intimate. If he's the one, all your fantasies and dreams will come to fruition in good time.

Keep It Hot!

Now that you've found a great guy and you're happy, and it's fun and sexy and new, new, new, why let that loving feeling end now that he's your boyfriend?

Date Night

Set aside one night per week when a shower and shaving your legs are mandatory and eating leftovers is not! For couples who have been together for twenty weeks or twenty months, date night will always be a fantastic way to create intimacy and privacy and excitement in any and all relationships. It's quiet time away from the kids, the house, and reality. Quality time to communicate and catch up, to enjoy each other and be reminded, yet again, of why you fell in love in the first place. Date night is your time to be pampered, your time to dress up, your time to feel good, and your time maybe even to get frisky.

Lingerie

Besides simply making you feel even more beautiful and sexy, lingerie will drive your man wild until the end of time. Men love and appreciate lingerie in a way that is indefinable, so surprise him from time to time and reap benefits both in the immediate and the unforeseeable future! Betty wears lingerie every chance she gets, and she loves the look of satin and lace. Her trademark garter belt is absolutely unforgettable.

Guy Time

If you've got date night nailed down, respecting his own time for his friends and his football should no longer be such a big deal. Be that girlfriend or wife who is not jealous or overly possessive. Letting your man do his thing will only keep you high atop his pedestal, the only place, after all, that you would ever want to be.

Betty Boop

Honest Love and True

Before you commit to *forever*, ask yourself the following questions:

1. Does he make you happy?
2. How does he treat his mother?
3. Do you share the same priorities?
4. Do your friends and family think he is good for you and to you?
5. Does he take care of himself? His health, his happiness, and his overall well-being?
6. Does he show you enough affection?
7. Does he think you're adorable?
8. Does he know how to say he's sorry?
9. Is he fiscally responsible?
10. If you want a family, does he?
11. Are you as much friends as you are lovers?
12. Does he support your goals and dreams? Is he your personal cheer-leader?
13. Can he handle pressure well?
14. Is he generous?
15. Is he honest?
16. Is he committed to you and to your relationship?
17. Does he have a good circle of quality people in his life? (You are the company you keep.)
18. Is he confident enough to give you space and allow you to do your own thing?
19. Do you suspect there are skeletons in his closet that you do not know about?
20. Does he love your furry companion or pet bird or fish?

Happy You and Merry Me

Beyond date night, lingerie, and guy time, there are a number of additional ways to make your longtime husband feel like your brand-new boyfriend forever and beyond. And vice versa, naturally. His perception is key, because sexy is a state of mind. A woman's age is irrelevant in this equation, as women will be sexy until the end of time. Knowing thyself is sexy. Wisdom is sexy. Confidence is sexy. Maintaining your girlishness is sexy. Being a loving and caring wife, mother, or grandmother is sexy. And maintaining your zest and zeal for life with all its pleasures is crucial. Whether she's biking or baking, dancing or laughing, posing or pouting, Betty's joie de vivre is ever present and utterly intoxicating. So, Boop away by keeping an open mind and sustaining your romantic spirit.

- Take a dance class together—ballroom, Latin, even hip-hop! The rewards are endless. Besides being a wonderful way to work out, it's a great activity to explore together. It's something to look forward to, to discuss, to practice, and to master. It will make the many celebratory invites you receive all the more exciting and fun and will, undoubtedly, ignite your love and passion.

- Dine with design. And by candlelight, for a change. Set the table with your very best china, bring fresh-cut flowers to the table, and get gussied up while you're at it. Just like lingerie, there is something innately romantic about the glow of a candle and the evening's quiet fresh breeze. Put some soothing tunes on your stereo and see where the evening takes you.

- Enhance your outdoor architecture. Invest in a porch swing or a hammock. Have a hot tub installed. You can quite easily and for very little expense create the trappings that chase your dreams.

Betty Boop

- Together, plan an extreme vacation where a passion or an activity or sport is the theme throughout. Take a challenging or thought-provoking tour rather than a prime spot at the pool and a take-out menu. Choose a destination that bears some kind of significance, be it spiritual, social, historic, or religious, and so on, and expand your horizons and your experiences. Just because you've never done something before doesn't mean that

the unfamiliar or uncharted won't be unbelievable in the end. Ask yourselves what you've always wanted to do, the sky's the limit, from skydiving to horseback riding, sailing, or backpacking. Let your adventurous spirit out, and the two of you will never be the same! Chartering new territory as a couple brings out and dusts off the feeling of firsts and newness in your relationship—guaranteed.

• If your free time is tight and your funds are even tighter, then a weekend spent at a lovely bed-and-breakfast in your outer area is a wonderful alternative to an exotic vacation. The quiet is natural, the privacy is innate, and best of all, there are no interruptions. Bunker down the entire time and snuggle to your heart's content, or choose an inn in a quaint town and explore.

• Tender loving care—personal attention and public affection like hand-holding and hugging. Even steal a kiss now and then!

Betty Boop

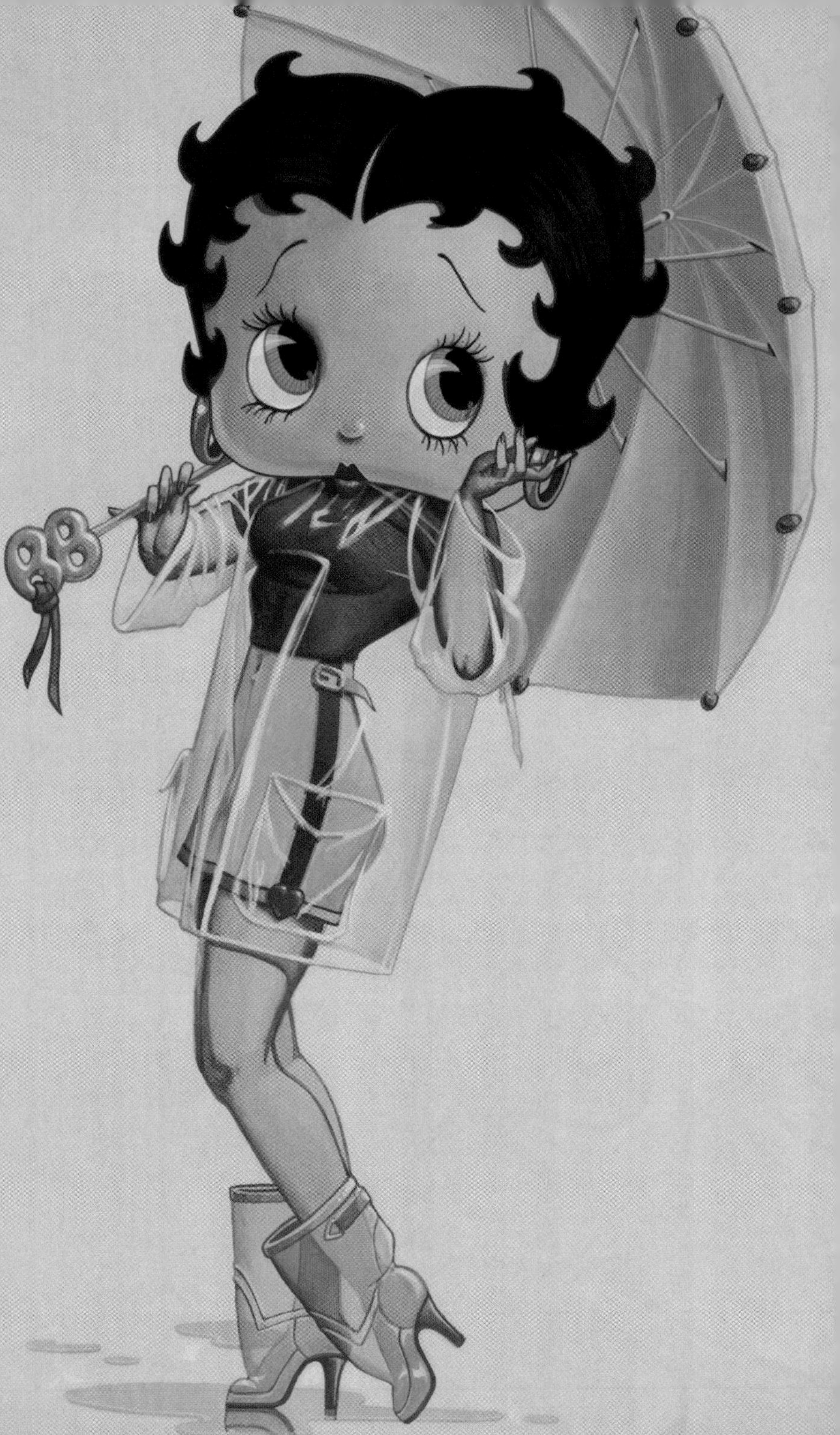

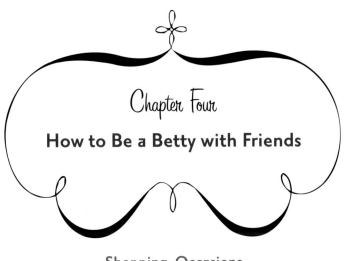

Chapter Four

How to Be a Betty with Friends

Shopping, Occasions

Friends! What would we do without them? Having good friends around you and keeping them over time are some of life's great pleasures.

Both new and old, our friends star in our favorite memories and support us through some of our worst challenges. Be it companionship, camaraderie, or a little bit of both, a lifetime with a handful of true friends is so comforting and all too sweet.

Betty Boop's free spirit makes her a great role model friendwise, as our friends should only add to our quality of life. Common interests and priorities, similar viewpoints and ethics, all these lend to the makings of the ultimate best friend.

Making Friends

Choose wisely. Unlike family relationships, our friendships are based solely on our own free will. Making friends and keeping them, as life gets serious, complicated, and hectic, are very important choices that every girl and woman will need to make. And maintaining those friendships so that they are honest and long-lasting is well worth the effort! So, be the kind of friend to others that you need and would want for yourself.

Cultivate the attributes you yourself are looking for in a true friend:

- *Be honest.* There is nothing lost or gained by pretending to be someone you're not. What is the advantage to disguising your dilemmas, hopes, and fears in front of those who you believe to be your trusted confidants? I can't think of any. Being real and keeping it real leads to wide-open lines of communication. Likewise, being able to put the brakes on a behavior or scenario in which a friend is doing something or saying something that makes you feel bad or uncomfortable, or worse, even hurt, is made all the more simple when you feel safe enough in that friendship to be honest.
- *Sacrifice.* Putting yourself first is ideal in theory and in the grand scheme of things, especially if and when what you want or need is vital or immediate and important enough that it can't wait.

Betty Boop

But for a friend, being there and supporting them through a rough patch or a huge moment should be paramount if not high atop your to-do list. When appropriate, going out of your way, being generous, and sacrificing for another means you can be the very best remedy to a friend in need, and it virtually guarantees the same effects in return. Immediate gratification is a dangerous desire when it comes to shopping, dessert, and boys, and so it goes that when it comes to friendships, there should be no such thing. Friends deserve patience and loyalty.

- *Listen.* "Stop, look, and listen" doesn't just apply to crossing the street. The same maneuver holds true with friendships. Being a good listener paves the way for your sage advice and your great if not groundbreaking observations. Your "shoulder skills" also speak volumes about how much you care about your friend and their well-being.

- *Cherish.* Treasure your friendships. Understanding how much they mean to you and how much pleasure they bring you should be enough for you to value your friends. If you haven't seen a friend, make and find the time to reconnect. Remember important dates and times in their lives, and send notes and cards or call to show you care. By treating your friendships in the way you would a flower, you will enable your relationships to bloom in full.

- *Flex.* Not just for Pilates, being a flexible friend is just as vital to

your core. So don't take change personally. A friend who cancels, who moves, who wants to switch plans, a date, a vacation; a friend who makes new ones, who dates a guy you don't fancy, or who builds a family without asking you first—all the change that the world has in store for you can't make your friendships falter. They may make them different, more complicated, or a little less available, but a good friendship is not based on quantity, but instead on quality. Have patience, understanding, and show grace. Good karma always comes full circle.

As the saying goes, "You are the company you keep," so the friendships we make and the friendships we maintain as we grow and as we change really need to be healthy, balanced, special, and so much fun!

Special Occasions

Will the duties of the best friend ever end? Nope! As the years progress, being the best friend will become a full-time gig! Enter warmings of all kinds, dinner parties, weddings and showers, baby number one, then two and three . . . The hostess with the mostess, the bridesmaid, the godmother . . . so many special occasions, so little time, and so many scenarios where one bad decision or one impromptu remark could become the headache of a lifetime.

Betty Boop

Love, Love, Love

From the bridesmaid's dresses to the name she's chosen for her first-born. From the wallpaper she's excited about for the guest room or what you really think of her in-laws, don't let your personal taste get in the way and cause a permanent stain on your friendship. Unless the issue is major and has the capacity to wreck the natural course of the universe, you are better off keeping those lingering thoughts in your head.

Dollars and Cents

Don't just think about that 401(k)—I'd consider starting a "friend-ship fund" and begin saving for the many bridesmaids' dresses that are in your future! The housewarming presents, the baby gifts, the celebratory dinners, and those unforgettable bachelorette bashes! *Très* expensive, but definitely tons of fun. Your best bet is to get creative when those friendly obligations come a-knockin'.

Tips and Ideas

- Plan bachelorette parties and big birthday trips and such way in advance and around national holidays or your allocated vacation days.
- Go in with friends on one big present rather than trying to show your love with a giant extravagant gift all on your own.
- Do some of those dinner parties and brunches at your home

rather than at a restaurant. Score big with thoughtful recipes, place cards, a soundtrack, flowers, a candle or two, and the important intimacy factor. Design cute invites, and dictate a dress code so lots of the trappings of a great time out with friends can be felt within those four familiar walls.

- Rather than shopping at retail for gifts, see what your crafty friends are up to. It's always great to buy original, one-of-a-kind creations. Think of it as supporting the arts or a budding entrepreneur rather than invigorating the swollen cash registers at a department store.

- If love is in the details, try a home-grown gift rather than a store-bought one. Spend some time and download music for personal CDs. You can create the soundtrack of your friendship, a heavenly rest-and-relaxation mix, or a ferocious cardio tape!

- Start vintage shopping for one-of-a-kind jaw-dropping presents! Find an authentic tour T-shirt from the first ever concert you experienced together or her very first celebrity crush. Present a vintage evening bag or clutch as a present. A retro watercolor or oil painting, something cute, sweet, or deco as a perfect housewarming gift. Or, best of all, a scrumptious and sexy Betty Boop T-shirt!

- Offer your own services—design a voucher or a gift certificate from the world of you. Some examples: Give a blowout,

Betty Boop

become a babysitter, or whip up her absolute favorite dish of yours and divulge the until-now secret recipe.

- Rather than going out and buying yet another fabulous frock for the occasion du jour, take one of your bridesmaid dresses to a local seamstress, and see if there's any hope. Turn a floor-length gown into a sexy cocktail dress or a great satin skirt. Go from fuchsia to black with dye. You'd be surprised at what you can come up with!

- Play photographer and snap photos at the festivities. Then, depending upon the occasion, create a frisky or endearing scrapbook as a belated gift. Scrapbooks complete with mementos, captions, and plenty of pictures taken "behind the scenes" make for the best presents, and when given, practically relive that special day or evening all over again.

- And this goes without saying: Being a Betty is as much about brains as it is about beauty. So, perhaps on this special occasion, why not indulge in your friend's intellectual side and gift-wrap a year's subscription to a national monthly magazine like *Time, Life,* or *National Geographic.* Or, buy her a book on the life of her favorite hero or heroine.

That's the greatest thing about girlfriends—there's no need to impress. All things that come from the heart will do just fine!

Betty Boop

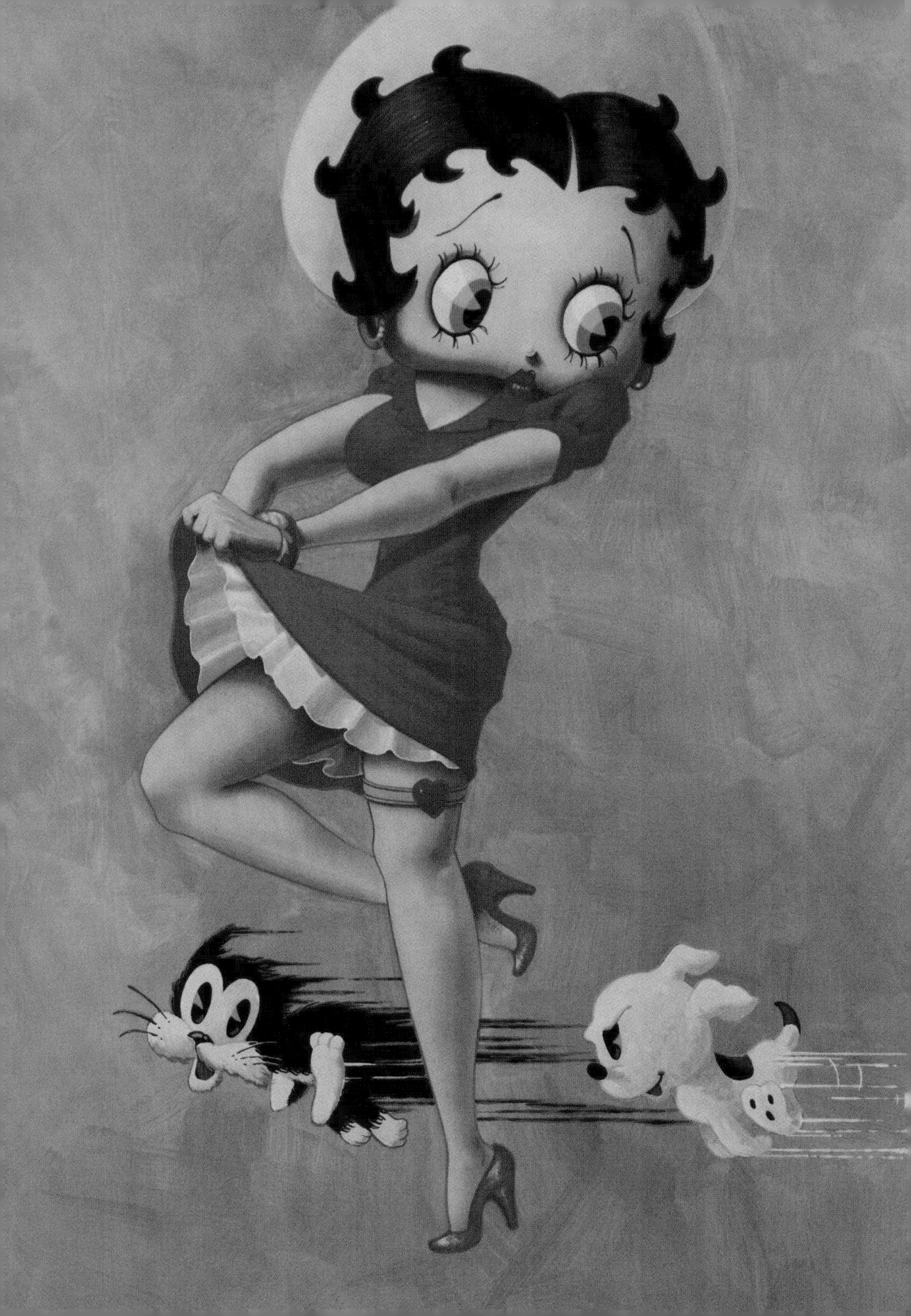

Chapter Five

How to Be a Betty at Home and with Your Family

Home is where the heart is—most of the time anyway! Family—love 'em or hate 'em, we can't live with 'em, and despite what we may want to believe from time to time, we just can't live without them. Between the history, the genetics, the safety, and the years' worth of drama, it's no doubt that when it comes to family, *complicated* just doesn't seem to do it all justice.

While all of us come from different worlds and households, different circumstances and relationships, in the end, we all just want to get along and make our families happy and proud.

That said, don't expect a quick fix on how to solve the age-old problems you have with your mom or how to deal with the brother-in-law you just can't find a single positive attribute for. Also, don't expect advice on how to make your mother-in-law finally understand that despite her paranoia, you are not following a plan to eliminate her from your lives. Don't look for insight into the sibling rivalry with your sister, who got the blue eyes in the family and left you with the brown.

However, there are a few Betty Boop–inspired pointers that, should you put the past behind you, promise to help you make the best of your present and help you add a little sunshine to your future. Betty's always been able to keep her calm even in the most elaborately strenuous of scenarios. She's the peacekeeper not the troublemaker. The art of maintaining grace under fire is just sentences away.

Atmosphere

Your best bet is to look at your home as your ally or accomplice. Consider your environment, and take inventory of the few small changes that you think are possible in order to level out any of the seismic waves that you register when your relatives step into it. From your kitchen to your closet, your decor and your behavior, when you're in your own home, look around and ask yourself what could possibly be done to alleviate an already tense situation. Then reflect on some of the semi-offensive "constructive criticisms" you've received over the years. Valid or not, try to determine whether you could stand to acquiesce in the name of good family relations and peaceful gestures.

Gestures

Here are some gestures that deep down inside you know won't really kill you.

- Frame their favorite or treasured family photo.
- Display the dreaded heirloom or hand-me-down that you otherwise can't bear to look at.
- Make the home-cooked meal even if your day or week has been a nightmare.
- Borrow or request the by now saintly family lasagna recipe, even though you love yours so much more.
- Organize your clutter, vacuum the carpets, let your bathrooms glisten, and put all the toys away. Turn your home into the family palace.
- Keep the conversations light. Save financial and relationship woes, friend's affairs, and uncomfortable parent–teacher conferences for when you close the door behind them.
- Use or don that Christmas present that you were so close to including in the garage sale you had last month.

It's not about letting them weigh in or whether they are right or wrong; it's about not giving them an inch of room to say or do another thing that could make the hair on your arms stand at attention yet again. And of course, it's about communication, in subtle unspoken ways that will let them know you care.

Betty Boop

The In-laws

A few helpful hints from women who've been there:

- Ring your mother-in-law once a week.
- Withhold information from your family that might make them jealous of one another or offend them. For instance, if you spent the afternoon at your parents' place rather than at your mother-in-law's, keep that to yourself.
- Invite a friend to join in the festivities—a non–family member—as a distraction or for the entertainment value.
- Get accustomed to hearing the same story more than once or twice or three hundred times.
- Get accustomed to laughing at those not-so-laughable jokes and remarks.
- From artwork to figurines to china, break it out when they visit.
- Make sure that every immediate family member is represented in the photo collection throughout your home.
- With regards to children, make sure holding time and playing time gets distributed evenly among family members.
- Keep them in the loop and updated versus asking them their opinion—from home decorating to baby names and schooling.
- From time to time, include your brother- and sister-in-law in your social circle if they demonstrate interest.
- Make sure that there is always an open bottle of wine.

Betty Boop

Balancing Act

Besides the hardships of family drama and being the happy wife and great mother, there's also the under-the-radar quotient of keeping it all together, being and staying (relatively) sane and happy. Maintain time for yourself and your own growth and enjoyment so that everything falls into place and that you succeed in all areas of your life.

Being one step away from crumbling to pieces or feeling like one of the many balls you've been juggling all this time is about to drop is no way to live. And, not surprisingly, ends up tarnishing all your other efforts. Thus, I've compiled a few general items that every woman needs to incorporate into her all-too-busy life for her very own sake.

Betty Boop

Housecleaning Blues

Not all of us are blessed with a fairy godmother or a weekly house-keeper, so because it's got to get done, do it as efficiently and as happily as you can.

- Invite a girlfriend over. Who said you can't do the dishes or fold the laundry as you're getting updated on all the latest gossip? Who knows, maybe she'll even help out.
- Find the reward. Treat yourself to a manicure the minute you've scrubbed the last toilet or put away the last dish. Something to look forward to.
- Consider housework as your allocated current-event symposium. By having the news stream in the background, it's like having a second set of hands. One set for chores and the other for your morning newspaper.
- If news is not your thing, put the radio on or a CD in that you haven't listened to for ages, and shake your groove thing and sing to the rafters while you pick up after everyone else.

Betty Boop

Swat That Fly

If a gorgeous landscaper isn't scheduled to trim your hedges anytime soon and if the majority of the responsibilities have been mysteriously allocated to you, here's your chance to make the best of it.

- Capitalize on the beautiful day, skip the hat and sleeves, dab on a bit of SPF-something to your nose and shoulders, and gain a nice healthy glow in the process.
- Change your outlook. Look at the day's responsibilities as another activity to get you out, moving, bending, pulling, and so forth.
- Take pride in the plants, flowers, and veggies you might be growing. Get as acquainted as you can with horticulture and agriculture, and turn a chore into a hobby.
- Bring your headset along and listen to your favorite music or chat with friends.
- Get your spouse or children (or both) interested. Make your outdoor chores a family affair, and celebrate with something yummy and sweet when you've conquered your tasks.

Betty Boop

Red-Hot Mama

If a mother isn't tending to her child, she's looking after them, she's worrying about them, and she's always hoping that she's doing the right thing. Since these questions are universal, here are some selected words of wisdom to aid you and ease your peace of mind.

1. Early on, you need to let go of your dream for what you feel your child should be. Allow yourself to see your child as an individual, independent of you. This way you will be better able to recognize their strengths and weaknesses and identify their interests and fears. With your parental eyesight at 20/20, you will be able to tend to and nourish your children in the very best ways. Being your child's advocate as well as their parent will enable you to help your child truly be the best version of themselves in their future.

2. Teach your child to be independent and *allow* them to be. Independence, at your teaching, will make them strong children, strong teenagers, and strong adults. It will bring a greater sense of trust to your evolving relationship and will only help you communicate honestly in the years to come.

3. Create boundaries. Instill a sense of privacy, tact, and respect in your child. Your child will prosper into a sensitive teenager who conducts themselves respectfully and treats others with respect, as well.

Betty Boop

4. Be consistent in your discipline. Work as a team with your husband or partner and maintain a united front. Send consistent messages, and maintain consistent standards.

5. Serve as your child's role model. You are your child's first love and their forever heroine, and they will learn their greatest life lessons from you. Being good to yourself should be a top priority.

6. Expose your children to all sorts of activities, from athletics to the arts to education. Allow them to flourish in the areas that they themselves determine, so that their self-worth and self-value extends beyond their looks and their status.

Betty Boop

You Time

It's not selfish; it's necessary. Showing your devotion to the ones you love doesn't mean that you should neglect yourself in the process. Carve time out for the following, make it work both from a time perspective and from a financial one, and enable yourself to become and remain a very happy camper so that that home of yours and that family can be a reward and not a burden.

- Schedule a spa day once a month or once a year—every woman deserves a little pampering!
- Discover a new passion or invigorate an old one.
- Start loving yourself, and quit smoking.

- Start loving your body by taking care of it, and lose those bothersome pounds.
- Make time for your girlfriends.
- TiVo or tape your favorite shows. Don't allow yourself to miss them.
- Still curious about a nagging subject matter or a seemingly elusive activity? Do your research, surf the Net, and find a way to examine and experience it.
- Energize a fading relationship with a family member, work colleague, or friend.
- Treat yourself to a mini makeover if you're feeling blah.
- Educate yourself. Become more familiar with technology or a subject matter that you've felt disconnected from or that you've always been curious about.
- Dive into a novel.
- Boop up your style! Whether you're walking the dog or tackling your grocery list, play dress-up. Betty would never dream of leaving the house looking like she just rolled out of bed. Getting dressed up is a Betty Boop ritual that only makes life and the everyday aspects of it all the more interesting and all the more fun.

Whatever it takes, ladies!

Betty Boop

Was the last time you had the girls over too long ago to recall? Upset that that expensive barbecue has become a dusty spiderweb-clad resting place for the local birdies? Disgruntled those family gatherings are never at your home? Have you been left feeling bad when your kids want to play at the neighbor's place instead of yours? Or just plain feeling disconnected?

Okay, here's the thing—if you don't extend the invites and maintain an environment that's conducive to various social scenarios, you've unwittingly dug your own hole. But don't fret. Here are some archived Betty Boop techniques that now are right at your fingertips:

- Host a cooking, knitting, book, or movie club at your place. Monthly, get your gal pals over to screen a just-released DVD or discuss Oprah's latest must-read, or sample new recipes that each of you have cooked up. Include your children or husbands when appropriate, and you'll soon see the social void in your life fulfilled.

- Birthday bashes. Go all out with great music, food, games, and semistocked bar. Who ever said that sweet sixteens were the only times we're supposed to get gussied up and celebrate our age? Share the spotlight with friends and families whose birthdays fall within the same window, and voilà, your house will be filled with laughter and tons of love.

- Age is just a number, so reinvigorate the costume party. Choose a theme, think up a quirky invite, drop the kids off with Mom, and live a little! Invite friends and neighbors, and get your social butterfly wings glued on tight. Don't wait for the "right" occasion—like New Year's or Halloween. Be a party innovator and think one up of your very own. It will be a welcome change of pace for your friends and family and will likely cure you of your lonely blues.

- Well in advance, claim a weekend or a holiday as yours. E-mail or inform friends and family by post that this year, on X date, you'd like them to usher in summer (for example) with you and your family. Cater if cooking is not your thing, make sure there's plenty of film in your camera, and bring in a bunch of flowers from that fanciful garden you've been slaving over all this time. Plan great activities and games, and see where the day or evening takes you. Who knows, your party could become an annual thing, or it may even cure you from ever wanting to be a hostess again.

Betty Boop

- If you've been tossing around the idea of a pool forever and ever, get over being practical, and go for it! It will increase the value of your property, provide wonderful downtime for your family, it may even get you to consider an aquatic workout, and it will definitely ensure that family and friends will be around a whole lot more.

- Modernize the traditional Tupperware party or reconnect with your community's Avon lady, and invite your gal pals over. From catalog gurus to your area's rising talents, jewelry and fashion to artists-in-training, hosting a gathering where your friends are introduced to the latest and greatest products, of all kinds, is an afternoon or evening that everyone will remember and thank you for.

All in all, if you think it up, make the effort, and extend yourself and your home, your social gripes will disappear, and your new mindset will spread. Keeping a happy home takes effort, but it will always be worthwhile.

Betty Boop

Boop-oop-a-doop!

Unarguably, Ms. Boop's unending and unmatched global appeal stems from her effervescence, her sweetness, and that sex appeal that just won't quit. And all of us, her admirers and her forever fans, have been captivated by her since the instant we met. She will always remind us of the best version of ourselves, our girlishness, the times we experienced our best emotions, sensations, and memories, and so our fondness for Ms. Boop will never fail. Being a little Betty-ish in our everyday lives, following her principles, and unleashing our own inner Boop is not only the best way to connect with our beloved icon, but it's also the most surefire and certain path to a life of sumptuous romance, endless adventure, and infinite Boop-oop-a-doops!

About the Author

Bronx-born SHERRIE KRANTZ grew up in New York and attended the University of Buffalo. She spent the first leg of her career as a public relations executive—first at Calvin Klein Inc., and then at Donna Karan International. From there, Sherrie founded Forever After Inc., parent company to www.Vivianlives.com, and cowrote *The Autobiography of Vivian: A Novel* and *Vivian Lives*. She continues to develop projects for television, film, and print and enjoys the company of her forever puppy, Stella. She resides in New York City.

About Betty Boop

BETTY BOOP was created by Max Fleischer on a drawing board during the dark days of the Great Depression and quickly became a legend as the first animated femme fatale. Since her 1930 debut, Betty Boop has starred in more than one hundred Fleischer cartoons, two syndicated comic strips, and two animated musical television specials for CBS. She was saluted in a prime-time, star-studded tribute on American Movie Classics and was the first cartoon character to be featured in A&E's award-winning Biography series. Today, with her unique combination of sassy spirit, sexual innocence, and common sense, she's become a citizen of the world and a role model for all women.